Essentials of elementary music Theory

by GEORGE RUSHFORD

RUBANK®

HAL•LEONARD®
CORPORATION

7777 W. BLUEMOUND RD. P.O. BOX 13819 MILWAUKEE, WI 53213

L-256

INTRODUCTION

The aim of this book is to present a plan that will enable students to learn the elements of music theory. No claim or attempt is made in offering new theories about music. Many books have been written on this subject but they have not been organized for the beginner so as to teach theory along with the progress made in playing an instrument.

The average instruction book used as a method for the various instruments does not contain enough material or complete explanations about music theory. Oral explanations are usually made by the teacher, yet even numerous repetitions often fail to be understood by students. With great numbers of players taking class work in public schools the instructor is not always able to check on each individual to find out if every point of theory is understood. By using a written plan the student is able to understand this subject better, and by grading the work of students, the teacher can find out what things are in need of more explanation.

Often students play correctly without knowing the names of notes. They play by ear and depend on other students for the time value of notes. Enharmonic notes continue to puzzle students long after they have passed the beginning stage of playing. An understanding of enharmonic notes will simplify the reading and fingering of a note. Scales are used by all musicians so an understanding of how they are constructed will make it easier to play them. An understanding of intervals and chord construction will enable players to perform better and gain a greater appreciation of what they are playing.

As this book progresses there is space for the student to write out what he is learning. This is a check to avoid the chance of merely reading the material over and still not understanding it. There is also additional space left for the instructor to write in any further explanation or practice needed by the individual student. A set of tests have been prepared covering the whole course. These should be given periodically and repeated by every student until all can get one hundred per cent on each test.

The busy teacher will save much time in addition to being certain that every student knows what he is playing. The student will not only know what a staff is; but also how and why it is made this way. Writing out these lessons will teach the student the names and fingerings of notes. Note values must be understood or the student can not fill in measures with correct time values of notes. Key signatures, enharmonic notes, transposition, intervals, scale and chord construction and other phases of elementary theory are all simplified and easily learned by covering this course.

GEORGE RUSHFORD

CONTENTS

ALPHABETICAL LISTING

ESSENTIALS OF ELEMENTARY MUSIC THEORY

Part I.

THE STAFF: ITS PARTS AND NOTES

Musical sounds are represented by characters called notes.

The notes are written on lines and spaces called a STAFF. Notes are named from the first seven letters of the alphabet—A, B, C, D, E, F, and G. The syllables used in singing are: Do, re, mi, fa, sol, la, ti.

A Staff is composed of five lines and four spaces.

Lines   Spaces

Draw STAFFS (STAVES) of five lines having four spaces.

Example

The lines and spaces above and below the staff are called LEGER LINES.

THE STAFF IS DIVIDED BY VERTICAL LINES CALLED BARS. Two lines are used at the end of a strain, or end of a selection; and this is a DOUBLE BAR.

The space between two bars is called a MEASURE.

Draw a staff and divide it into four measures, with a double bar at the end.

1.

Make a second staff and divide it the same way.

2.

Draw a staff and divide it into eight measures, with a double bar at the end of the fourth measure and also a double bar at the end of the last measure.

1.

Make another staff and divide it the same way. Add **leger lines**.

2.

Divide the staffs on page 5 into measures, placing a double bar at the end of each staff.

A CLEF SIGN is placed at the beginning of a staff or strain to determine the pitch of notes.

The G CLEF (treble) determines that G is on the second line and other notes are determined in relation to it because it is built on the 2nd line G.

The F CLEF (bass) determines that F is on the fourth line.

With the movable C Clef the note C is determined by the position of the clef sign. The viola or alto clef usually places middle C on the third line.

The Tenor Clef is placed on the fourth line and is sometimes used for the cello and bassoon.

Steps in making a G (treble) Clef sign.

Practice making G Clef signs.

Steps in making an F (bass) Clef sign.

The ALTO CLEF is generally simplified in manuscript writing.

Make ten CLEF SIGNS (any kind).

Notes are written in various shapes depending on the length of time a note is to be sounded. A whole note (○) is not made with just a round circle, but with two half circles. Ex. ○

Make a line of whole notes:

A HALF NOTE is made the same as a whole note with the addition of a stem. If the stem points upward the stem is on the right side of the note: (♩) If the stem points downward the stem is on the left side of the note. (♩) Notes below the third line have the stems pointing upward and notes above the third line have the stems pointing downward. Notes on the third line may have the stems pointed either upward or downward.

Make a row of half notes with stems pointing upward on some of the notes, and downward on the others. The length of a stem on a note is about $2\frac{1}{2}$ spaces on a staff. Notes written out of the staff or notes requiring connecting bars usually have the stem somewhat longer.

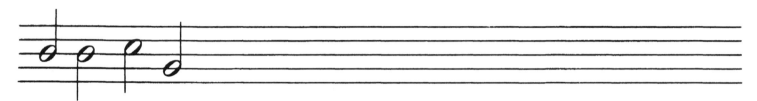

QUARTER notes and other filled-in notes are often made with one stroke of a special broad point writing pen. ● ♩ ♩ As a note made in this manner may be too small to be read easily, many prefer to fill in notes with strokes as used in making whole or half notes. ○ ♩ ○ ♩

Make a row of quarter notes. ♩ ♩

The addition of one or more lines (flags) on a quarter note will change it to a note of different time value.

Write additional notes as the examples.

The position of the notes on the staff determine their pitch and letter names. Notice that when we get to G we start again on A.

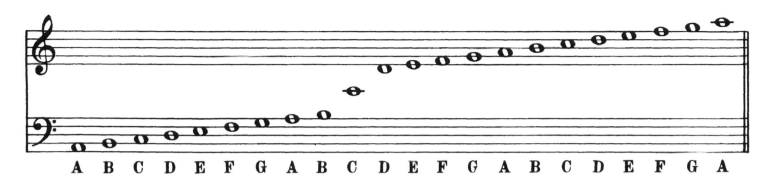

A B C D E F G A B C D E F G A B C D E F G A

Why notes do not have the same names for all clefs. In early music-writing the notes were written on a GREAT STAFF of eleven lines.

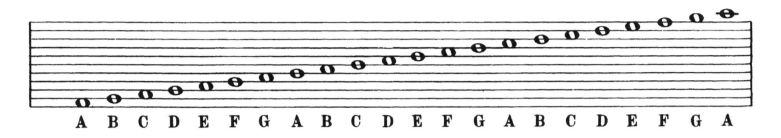

A B C D E F G A B C D E F G A B C D E F G A

As the use of so many lines made music somewhat difficult to read, the staff was divided, causing lines and spaces to have different names for the different clefs.

Clefs placed on the great staff divide it as follows: The staffs of three different clefs derived from the grand staff but they are used as separate staffs now.

A B C D E F G A B C D E F G A B C D E F

Part II.
NOTE NAMES AND NOTE SPELLING

Make a clef sign and write a note above each letter name in the staff below. Write the fingering or position for the instrument you play, as cornet, violin, trombone, etc.

C E B A C F E D E C F F

Write the name and fingering under the following notes.

Practice space.

C D E F G A B C

A B C D E F G A

C D E F G A B C D E

Write notes on the staff corresponding to the letter name for the words written below. Refer to the clef used for the instrument you play. Place a clef sign before each word.

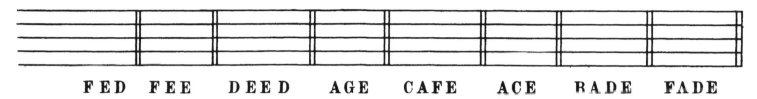

FED   FEE   DEED   AGE   CAFE   ACE   BADE   FADE

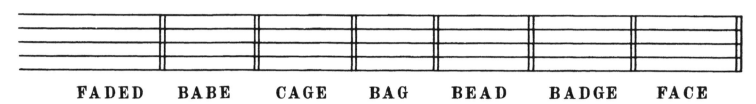

FADED   BABE   CAGE   BAG   BEAD   BADGE   FACE

Place the fingering under the notes, if you play an instrument as cornet, clarinet, violin, etc.
Make up additional words.

Write the letter name under each note to spell out words.

Also place the fingering under the notes for the instruments you play.

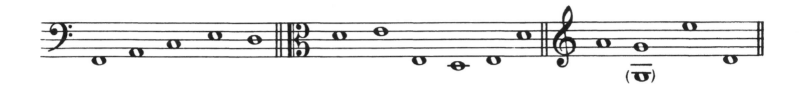

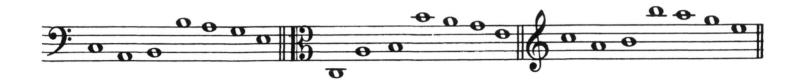

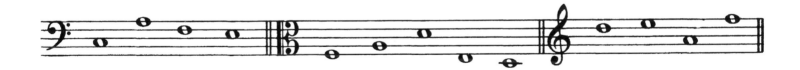

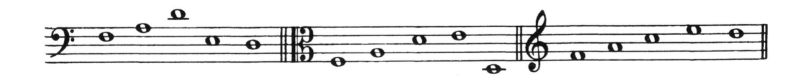

Write the words "fade" and "cabbage" on the staff in as many ways as possible. Write other words in various ways.

Part III.

TIME SIGNATURES AND NOTE VALUES

As previously stated the length of time a note is sounded depends on the kind of a note it is and value given to it by the time signature.

Whole note **o**   Half note   Quarter note

Whole rest   Half rest   Quarter rest

Time signature.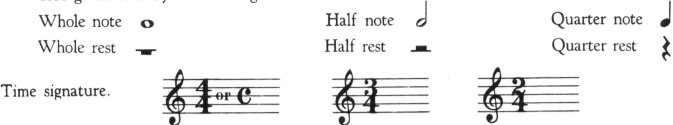

The top number tells how many beats there are in each measure and the bottom number tells what kind of a note receives one beat. Common time (**C**) is considered the same as 4/4.

A **rest** is a period of silence.

In 4/4 time a **o** or a receives four beats; a or receives two beats; a or receives one beat.

A half rest () looks like a hat right side up; a whole rest () looks like a hat up-side down. It will be helpful to remember a whole rest as resembling a hat up-side down as it will hold more that way.

Place bars in the correct places to conform to the time signature. Ex.
o
1 2 3 4 | 1 2 3 4 | 1

Place counts under the notes.

Complete the measures so that they contain the right number of beats.

A dot (.) placed after a note increases it by one-half of its value.

Ex. 𝅗𝅥   𝅗𝅥 .   𝅗𝅥.

½ of 2 = 1   1   2 + 1 = 1 2 3

Add whatever notes or rests are necessary to complete the measures for 3/4 time.

3/4 𝅗𝅥 | 𝅗𝅥. | 𝅗𝅥 | 𝅘𝅥 | | | | ‖

Fill in measures as many ways as possible and place counts under the notes and rests.

1. 4/4	3/4	2/4
2.		
3.		
4.		
5.		
6.		
7.		
8.		
9.		
10.		

Part IV.

SHARPS, FLATS, ACCIDENTALS, KEY SIGNATURES

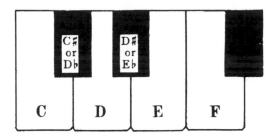

From one key to the next is one half step.

A flat (♭) lowers the pitch of a note one half step.

A double flat (♭♭) lowers a note two half steps.

A sharp (♯) raises the pitch of a note one half step.

A double sharp (𝄪) raises a note two half steps.

A natural (♮) cancels a sharp or a flat.

Two naturals are necessary to cancel a double flat (♭♭) or double sharp (𝄪). A natural (♮) and a sharp (♯) will cancel one sharp after a note has been affected by a double sharp. A natural (♮) and a flat (♭) will cancel one flat after a note has been affected by a double flat.

Sharps or flats indicating the key are called the **Key Signature**.

The key signature affects notes of the same name throughout the strain or selection even though they are on different degrees of the staff.

An accidental is a sharp or flat found in the music but not in the key signature. It affects the note or notes on the same line or space, only through the measure in which it appears.

Place a sharp or flat before the notes affected by the key signature.

Write in the names and fingerings of the notes.

Part V.

EIGHTH NOTES, EIGHTH RESTS, METHOD OF COUNTING TIME

An eighth note (♪) is equal in time value to one half of a quarter note. As a quarter note re-ceives one beat in 4/4 time, an eighth note will receive a half beat.

An eighth rest (♇) is a period of silence having the same time value as an eighth note.

If an eighth note receives ½ beat, how many eighth notes does it take to equal one beat? ....

How many eighth notes are needed to equal 2 beats? ....

How much time does an eighth note (♪) and an eighth rest (♇) equal? ....

Eighth notes and eighth rests are usually counted in the following way:

A way to count eighth notes (and other notes) accurately, is to the beat of the foot by playing an eighth note on the down beat (↓) of the foot and the following half beat on the up beat (↑) of the foot.

This also applies to notes of other time values.

Ex.

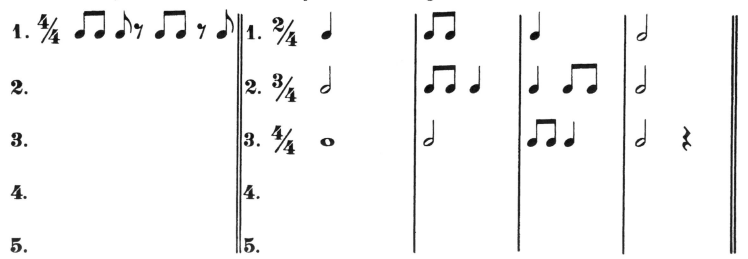

Write eighth notes and rests in various ways.

1.

2.

3.

4.

5.

Complete the following measures.

1.

2.

3.

4.

5.

Place down and up beats and the counts under the notes.

Part VI.
THE TIE, SLUR, DOT, REPEAT SIGN, NOTE READING

A tie () is a curved line connecting two adjoining notes on the same degree of the staff. The notes tied are sounded as one note and held for the total number of beats of the notes contained in the tie.

Since a dot (.) increases a note by one half of its value, a note receiving one beat (♩) will receive one and a half beats if a dot is placed after it.

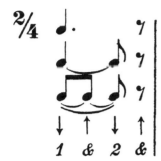

Fill in measures making use of dotted notes.

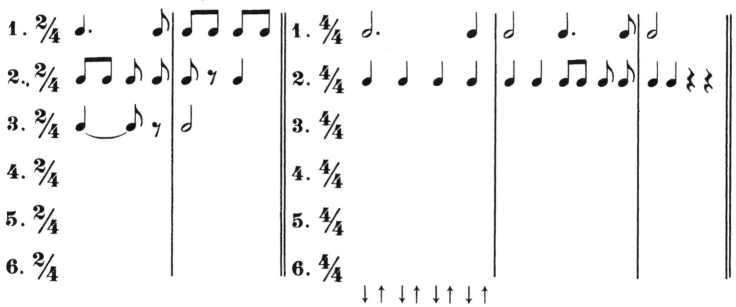

Notes in each of the above measures must total 2 beats.

Notes in each of the above measures must total four beats.

A slur is a curved line () joining notes on different degrees of the staff. Slurred notes are played or sung smoothly with one breath. In the case of string instruments, slurred notes are played while the bow moves in one direction.

REPEAT SIGN.
Two dots at the end of a strain signify that the strain is to be played over again.

Dots on both sides of a double bar show that the strain to the left of the bar is to be repeated and the strain following is also to be repeated starting with the notes at the right of the repeat sign.

Most music is written within the staff. The notes on the added lines and spaces (leger lines) should be given special attention so that these notes in the extreme high or low registers are as easily read as those within the staff.

Write words using notes in the register most useful to you.

If you play an instrument requiring fingering, as the cornet, violin, clarinet, etc., write the fingering under the note also. (Refer to a fingering chart if necessary.)

We learned in an earlier lesson that the first seven letters of the alphabet are used to name notes. When we get to the eighth letter we start over again.

1	2	3	4	5	6	7	8
A	B	C	D	E	F	G	A
B	C	D	E	F	G	A	B
C	D	E	F	G	A	B	C

Part VII.

INTERVALS

An INTERVAL is the difference in pitch between two tones. Intervals are counted upward from the lowest tone and include the note above.

Ex.   A to B is a second.   A to C is a third.

A to F is a sixth.   B to D is a third (3 letters included—B, C, D,).

A to A is an OCTAVE—a word meaning eight.

If A to A or any interval is on the same degree of the staff, this is called a PRIME (the Italian word for "first.")   Ex.

Prime   Octave

What are the following intervals?

3rd

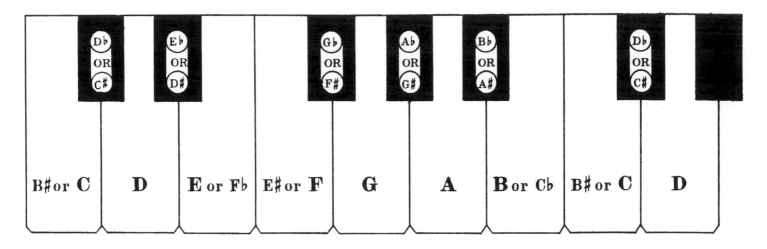

From one key to the next is one half step.   Ex. C to C♯; B to C.

From any key to a third key is a whole step (2 half steps). Ex.: C to D. — E to F♯.

WHY ONE KEY MAY HAVE TWO DIFFERENT LETTER NAMES

A sharp (♯) raises a note a half step, C raised to the next key above (to the right) would be called C♯. By lowering D one half step, D♭ would fall on the same key as C♯. Thus we find that C♯ and D♭ have the same pitch. E♯ sounds the same as F, and F♭ sounds the same as E. Notes written on different degrees of the staff, but which sound alike, are called **enharmonic tones**.

From E to G there are three half steps but the interval is referred to as a step and a half. There are four half steps from C to E, and this interval is considered as two whole steps.

How many steps are there between the following notes?

C to C♯? ....   C to E? ....

A to B? ....   E♭ to G? ....

E to F? ....   F♯ to G♯? ....

B to C? ....   B♭ to C? ....

F♯ to G? ....   F to A? ....

G♭ to G? ....   F to A♭? ....

Part VIII.

SIGNS AND ABBREVIATIONS

SIGNS AND ABBREVIATIONS USED IN MUSIC

Prima Volta—First time. Second Volta—Second time.

Play the 1st ending the first time and repeat; the second time skip the first ending and go to the second ending.

Dal Segno (Dalseyo) D. S. — go back to the sign: 𝄋

Play to fine (fee-ney) — end, conclusion, finis. 𝄐 Pause-stop.

Da Capo — D. C. From the beginning.

Coda. An added passage — Final movement.

Coda Sign. ⊕ Skip to the Coda after D. S. or D. C.

𝄐 Fermata — To pause or hold.

Fine

D.S.

Sign to repeat as ⫽ previous measure   4—rest four meas-ures.   8—rest eight meas-ures.   Play 4 eighth notes.   Play 4 sixteenth notes.

Part IX.

SIXTEENTH NOTES, SIXTEENTH RESTS AND COMPARATIVE NOTE VALUES

A sixteenth note (𝅘𝅥𝅯) is a note having two flags. A sixteenth note is 1/16 part of a whole note. It takes sixteen sixteenth notes to equal a whole note. Four sixteenths equal a quarter note.

How many sixteenth notes (𝅘𝅥𝅯) equal a half note? (𝅗𝅥) ....

How many sixteenth notes (𝅘𝅥𝅯) equal a quarter note? (𝅘𝅥) ....

How many sixteenth notes equal an eighth note? (𝅘𝅥𝅮) ....

A sixteenth rest (𝄿) is a period of silence equal in time value to a 16th note (𝅘𝅥𝅯)

Complete the following measures placing the notes in position corresponding to correct time values.

5.

6.

7.

8.

9.

10.

Dotted eighth notes and dotted eighth rests.

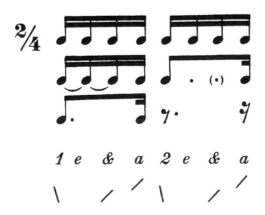

1 e & a 2 e & a

down up a down up a

Two dots increases a note by three fourths of its value.

Part X.
SCALES

MAJOR AND CHROMATIC SCALES AND KEY SIGNATURES

A scale is a succession of tones ascending or descending, according to a specified pattern, from a given note to its octave. A scale may continue beyond a single octave.

A chromatic scale is a progression of notes a half step apart. To avoid using more accidentals (♯'s or ♭'s) than necessary, a chromatic scale is usually written in the following way:

Ascending	Descending
C C♯ D D♯ E F F♯ G G♯ A A♯ B C	B B♭ A A♭ G G♭ F E E♭ D D♭ C

Make a staff and write in the above chromatic scale. Write the fingering under each note for the instrument you play.

Write Chromatic Scales starting on the following notes.

1. A

2. G

3. D

4. E♭ downward first, then up.

5. B♭ downward first, then up.

A **MAJOR SCALE** of one octave is built according to the following pattern: (See piano keyboard—Scale of C).

1st to 2nd tone—whole step;
2nd to 3rd tone—whole step;
3rd to 4th tone—half step;
4th to 5th tone—whole step;
5th to 6th tone—whole step;
6th to 7th tone—whole step;
7th to 8th tone—half step;

The eight tones of a major scale have half steps (∧) between the 3rd and 4th tones and the 7th and 8th tones. The other tones have whole (—) steps between them. EX. 1 — 2 — 3∧4 — 5 — 6 — 7∧8.

The first half of a major scale has exactly the same interval pattern as the upper half: Whole step, whole step, half step. This pattern of notes is called a **tetra-chord.**

Sharps will appear in various scales in the following order.

Flats appear in the key signature in the order written below.

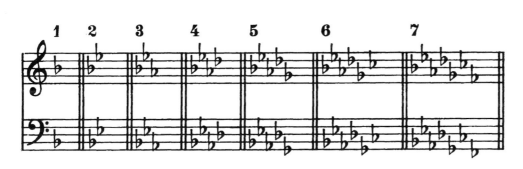
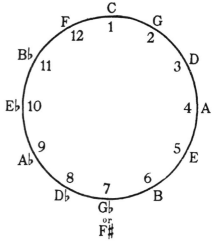

Circle of keys.

Starting with the scale of C Major the fifth note of each scale is used as the key note for the following scale.

The scale of C MAJOR does not require any sharps or flats in the key signature to make helf steps between the third and fourth and the seventh and eighth tones.

Build Major Scales on the notes given below. A scale is named from the note it starts on.

Place sharps in the key signature so as to make half steps between the third and fourth and seventh and eighth tones. The other tones will then have whole steps between them. The seventh tone of a major scale is always the new sharp.

1. G Major

2. A Major

3. E Major

4. D Major

5. F♯ Major

6. B Major

7. C♯ Major

28

Build major scales starting on the notes given below. Write flats in the key signature in proper order where they are required. The fourth tone of a major scale is always the new flat.

1. F Major

2. Eb Major

3. Bb Major

4. Db Major

5. Ab Major

6. Cb Major

7. Gb Major

Part XI.

TRANSPOSITION

When a note is played on a piano, oboe, violin, C flute, C saxophone, or any other C instrument, the note will sound as it is written. (A few instruments will sound an octave higher or lower.)

Instruments as the Bb cornet, Bb clarinet, Bb saxophone and other Bb instruments, will sound one note lower than written as compared to a piano or other C instrument. For this reason music is written one step higher for Bb instruments than for instruments in C.

This does not apply to instruments played in the F clef (bass clef). Instruments played in the F Clef will sound as written (or an octave lower) regardless of what key the instrument is built in.

When C is played on an Eb instrument using the G clef, the note will sound Eb. This is a step and a half higher, or four and a half steps lower than the note is written.

The following will sound the same when played by instruments playing in the key designated.

Bb Instruments

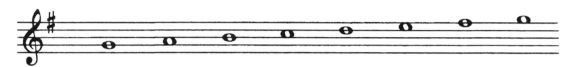

C Instruments

Eb Instruments

Db Instruments

F Instruments

Write notes for B♭ and E♭ instruments to sound the same as notes written for C instruments. Place the names and fingerings under the notes.

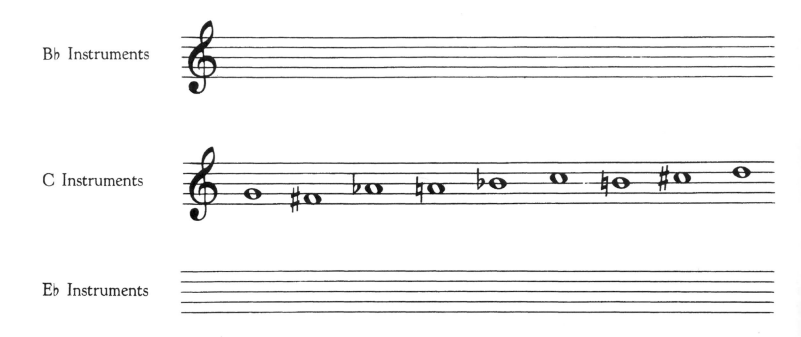

Instead of transposing C music for a B♭ instrument one step higher it is possible to transpose five whole steps lower. (A major seventh—see intervals, page 16.)

Music for E♭ instruments may be transposed four and a half steps higher than C music. These transpositions will cause the notes to sound in a different octave, otherwise the notes have the same letter names as the preceding transpositions.

Transpose the following five steps lower (a 7th) for B♭ instruments. Compare it with the preceeding transposition.

Transpose the following notes for E♭ instruments by writing them four and a half steps higher. (Major sixth—see intervals.)

E♭ Instruments

C Instruments

Transpositions may be made to any note, as a half step higher, half step lower; three and a half steps higher, (5th higher) three steps lower (4th), etc. One of the most useful transpositions is an octave higher or octave lower. This transposition is valuable to players of any musical instrument. Instruments built in D♭ transpose one half step lower than music written for instruments in C; F instruments sound a fourth higher or fifth lower than C instruments and transpositions should be made accordingly.

WHY INSTRUMENTS ARE BUILT IN VARIOUS KEYS

Music would sound very uninteresting if all brass instruments, wood-wind, and other instruments had the same tone quality. To get different tone quality or tone color, instruments are made in different sizes. When instruments are made in different sizes they have a definite pitch and are classified as E♭, B♭, C, F, instruments, etc. The key is determined in relation to the pitch of the notes sounded in comparison to a piano or other C instruments.

WHY ALL INSTRUMENTS DO NOT SOUND NOTES AS THEY ARE WRITTEN

As we have instruments made in various keys to give different tone colors, a problem of fingering comes up. A played on a B♭ instrument will sound as G on the piano: The note A played on an E♭ instrument will sound as C on the piano. If notes were fingered as they sound instrument players would have to use different fingering every time they wished to play an instrument built in a different key. A musician can play saxophones in the key of C, B♭, or E♭ and the fingering is the same on all of them. This remains true for playing other wood-wind instruments as the oboe, flute, clarinet, etc. On most of these instruments the note A is played by covering the two top holes, B is played by covering the top hole, G is played by covering three holes.

Brass instruments having three valves are played very much alike, as the cornet, E♭ alto horn, bass horns, horns in F, etc.

Part XII.

DYNAMICS AND TEMPO

Forte—F.—Loud
Mezzo Forte—mf.—Medium loud.
Fortissimo—ff—Very loud.

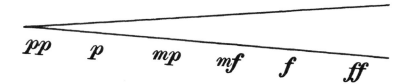

Piano—p—Soft.
Mezzo Piano—mp—Medium soft.
Pianissimo—pp—Very soft.

This sign ∧ or > placed over or under a note indicates that the note marked is to be accented or emphasized. Sforsando or forzando (fort-san-do) sfz. indicates that a note is to be very strongly accented, regardless of how loud or soft you are playing.

Crescendo (Cray-shen-do) (cresc.)   Decrescendo ⸱ ⸱ Diminuendo
                                                      decresc.   dim.

Gradually growing louder.   Gradually getting softer.

A dot placed above or below a note ♩ ♩ indicates that the note is to be played staccato. (De-tached—Separated) ♪̇ = ♪ 𝄾

Dashes placed under or over notes show they are to be played smoothly or in a broad manner. ♩ ♩ ♩

A curved line over a phrase indicates the phrase is to be played smoothly.

TEMPO

Tempo is the relative speed a number is to be played, according to the character of the composition.

A METRONOME is a mechanical instrument which can be regulated to tick at a desired speed notes are to be played. M.M. —90 indicates that the metronome is set to tick at a speed for playing ninety quarter notes per minute.

Moderato—Moderate tempo.

Allegro (al-lay-gro)—fast.

Allegretto——A little fast.

Agitato—Agitated.

Vivace (Vee-vah-chay) fast——lively.

Presto— Rapid.

Maestoso—Majestically.

Marcato—Marked—emphasized.

Andante—Slowly—gracefully—to walk.

Andantino—Not quite as slow as andante.

Adagio—Slow.

Ritardando—(Rit.) (ree-tar-dan-do) Slacken or diminish speed (not volume).

Rallentando—(Rall.)—Gradually becoming slower.

These words are some of the most commonly used to indicate speed or changes of music tempo. It is necessary to refer to a dictionary to become acquainted with all the terms used by composers.

Additional words:

34

Part XIII.
RHYTHM, METER, AND SYNCOPATION

Time in music is the duration value given to notes. Time and rhythm are closely related but they are not the same. Rhythm is expression given to music, in addition to correct time value given to notes. When rhythm can be reduced to an absolute rule where the accents occur regularly, it ceases to be rhythm and becomes meter. METER is the measurement of time by regular recurrence of impulse or accents. Music, even though played in correct time, but without measured expression is as uninteresting as listening to some one reading in a monotone.

A measure of **duple meter** has an accented beat (—) followed by an unaccented beat (◡)

A measure of **triple meter** has an accented beat (—) followed by two unaccented beats.

A **simple measure** has **one** of these meter units.

A compound measure has two meter units. The first unit receives the strongest accent called the primary accent. The emphasis placed in the second unit is called the secondary accent.

Duple
Compound

Triple
Compound

Frequently a piece starts with an incomplete measure.

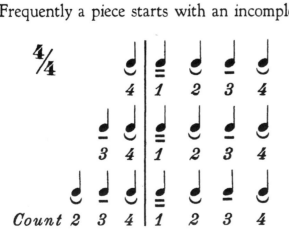

The remaining beats necessary to fill out a complete measure are usually found at the end of a strain or piece.

Bars are an aid in reading music by grouping the meter units within measures.

A meter unit may be altered for a special effect by placing the emphasis on different beats.

SYNCOPATION

SYNCOPATION is the displacement of accent causing irregular rhythm. An accent now occurs on that part of a measure not usually accented.

Ex.

The value of one beat may be given to various kinds of notes. The top number tells how many beats in each measure and the bottom number designates what kind of note will receive one beat.

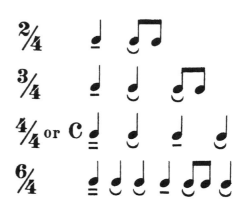

A compound measure has two or more meter units.

It is possible to have a measure contain duple and triple meter.

Ex.

Examine some music scores to find the strong and weak beats.

Part XIV.

COUNTING 6/8 TIME

In 6/8 measure there are six beats to a measure and an eighth note, or eighth rest, receives one beat. In rapid 6/8 time, two beats are counted to each measure, each set of three 8th notes being played as a triplet.

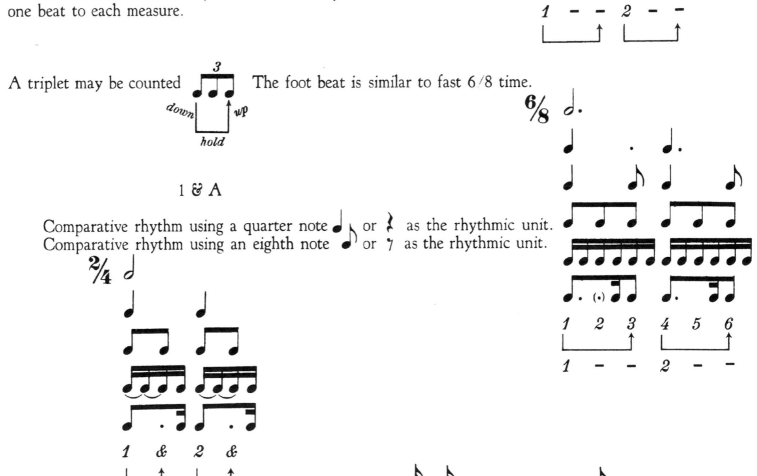

In counting rapid 6/8 measure to the beat of the foot, the foot goes down on the count of one; is held down for the count of two; and is raised on the count of three. Counts 4, 5, and 6, are played in the same manner.

Comparison of counting 6/8 measure.

Waltzes are written in 3/4 measure and may be counted out one beat to each measure.

A triplet may be counted   The foot beat is similar to fast 6/8 time.

1 & A

Comparative rhythm using a quarter note ♩ or 𝄽 as the rhythmic unit.
Comparative rhythm using an eighth note ♪ or 𝄾 as the rhythmic unit.

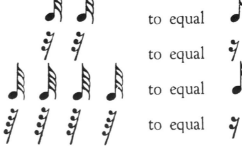

A thirty-second note has three flags. It takes two   to equal

A thirty-second rest has three flags. It takes two   to equal

A sixty-fourth note has four flags. It takes four   to equal

A sixty-fourth rest has four flags. It takes four   to equal

Part XV.

EMBELLISHMENTS AND NOTE GROUPING

A **triplet** is a group of three notes equal in time value to two of its kind.

A **quintuplet** is a group of five notes equal in time value to four or six of its kind.

A **sextuplet** is a group of six notes equal in time value to four of its kind. (This is proportionate to two triplets.)

A **septuplet** is a group of seven notes equal in time value to four or six of its kind equal in value to

A **nonuplet** is a group of nine notes played or sung in the time of six or eight of its kind equal in time value to

The above notes are grouped in uneven numbers. The note on the count following the group will form a balanced rhythm. It is generally preferable to feel the rhythm of these groups rather than count an exact division of the notes.

A **cadenza** is a group of notes sometimes introduced at the close of a phrase.

The first four notes are usually taken rather slowly with the first one accented. The following notes are played ad libitium, with accents following on notes of importance as to harmony. The cadenza may be accelerated or retarded in parts so as to form a balanced rhythm.

EMBELLISHMENTS

Embellishments are represented by various figures. They are ornamentations elaborating music and are built around a note in a melody. A **grace note** is a small note preceding a main note. The grace note has no time value of its own but takes time from the main note.

Written   Played

Double or **triple grace** notes may precede a main note. In all cases the grace notes are played very quickly, and the accent falls on the main note.

A **trill** is made by alternating a main note with a note a whole or half step above.

A trill should be played evenly and as rapidly as possible. The trill may be accelerated or retarded.

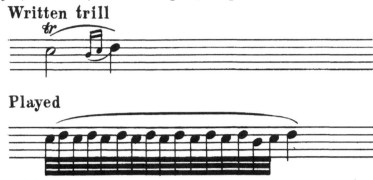

A **mordent** is played by playing a main note followed by a note above or a note below.

(a) Mordent.   (b) Inverted mordent.

Number 1 TURN (∾) is played by sounding a main note, the note above, the main note, note below, and the main note again.

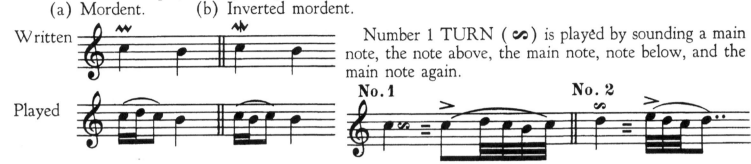

Part XVI.

MINOR SCALES - SCALE WRITING

A MINOR SCALE is built on a note a step and a half (minor third) lower than a relative major scale having the same key signature.

Where are the half steps in a major scale?

The half steps in a major scale are between the ....

The Harmonic Minor scale has half steps between the second and third, the fifth and sixth, and the seventh and eighth notes. There is a step and a half (1½) between the sixth and seventh tones.

In the Melodic Minor the sixth and seventh tones are raised one half step ascending, and lowered again in descending. This makes the half steps between the second and third tones, and the seventh and eighth tones ascending. In descending, the melodic minor has the half steps between the sixth and fifth and also between the third and second tones.

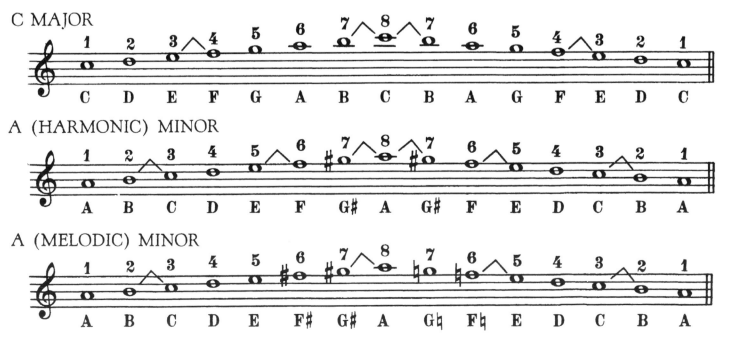

Write the following scales and place the necessary sharps in the key signature.

G   Major scale having 1 sharp.

Harmonic minor scale having 1 sharp.

Melodic minor scale having 1 sharp.

D   Major scale — 2 sharps.

Harmonic minor scale — 2 sharps.

Melodic minor scale — 2 sharps.

A   Major scale — 3 sharps.

Harmonic minor scale — 3 sharps.

Melodic minor scale — 3 sharps.

E   Major Scale — 4 sharps.

Harmonic minor scale — 4 sharps.

Melodic minor scale — 4 sharps.

F   Major scale — 1 flat.

Harmonic minor scale — 1 flat.

Melodic minor scale — 1 flat.

B♭   Major scale — 2 flats.

Harmonic Minor scale — 2 flats.

Melodic minor scale — 2 flats.

Eb   Major scale — 3 flats.

Harmonic minor scale — 3 flats.

Melodic minor scale — 3 flats.

Ab   Major scale — 4 flats.

Harmonic minor scale — 4 flats.

Melodic minor scale — 4 flats.

Part XVII.

CONDUCTING

An understanding of how a leader directs with a baton will better enable the players in a band or orchestra to play together correctly.

One of the first and most important things for performers to consider is to give undivided attention to the director. Without discipline and order no musical organization can accomplish much.

As soon as the director comes before the group everyone should look forward and listen for instructions. There should be no talking, playing of instruments, or noise of any kind. At rehearsals there are many humorous situations the director will bring to attention without several groups carrying on separate disturbances.

When the director steps on the podium to start the band or orchestra all instruments should be in ready position. In the absence of a podium or in a delay between numbers the baton may be rested on the stand. As the director takes the baton from the stand all instruments should be in ready position as follows: Players of cornet, trumpet, and trombones should have the bell of the instrument resting on the left knee with the mouthpiece pointing straight upward. Flutes may also be rested perpendicular on the left knee. Violins and violas should be rested with the end pin on the left knee with the strings away from the player and the left hand on the neck of the instrument in playing position. The oboe, clarinets, and English horn are placed in readiness with the bell resting on the right knee. Players should have hands in playing position on the French horn, baritone, bassoon, and saxophones. These last mentioned instruments and even the bass horn should have the mouthpiece several inches away from the mouth so they and all instruments can be brought in playing position at the precise instant the director raises the baton for the first note.

The director who raises the baton before first having the players' attention and instruments in readiness will find a very awkward pause before all players have the instruments in playing position.

DIRECTING

It will be much easier to follow the director if the direction of the baton for various beats is understood.

HOW TO HOLD THE BATON

The baton is held between the tip of the index and second finger and held in place by the thumb. The lower part of the baton is against the palm of the hand. The beats are conducted by a combined motion of the wrist and forearm.

DIRECTION OF THE BATON

There is always a little warning stroke called the cue beat before the first beat of a selection.

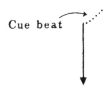

Beats as given by   Beats shown
the director.   facing director.

The count of "one" is always a down stroke. The first count is also a little more vigorous than the other beats.

Two beats to a measure is a down stroke on count one and an up-stroke on count two. 6/8 time may be counted two beats to each measure.

In four beats to each measure the baton comes down on count "one," and count "two" is to the left of the director (right of player). Count "three" is to the right; and count "four" the baton is brought back to the starting point.

The baton follows the general outline of a triangle in three beats to each measure.

9/8 time can be directed as three beats to each measure and 12/8 can be directed as four beats to each measure. Compound time as 5/4 can be directed as two measures one having three beats and one of two beats.

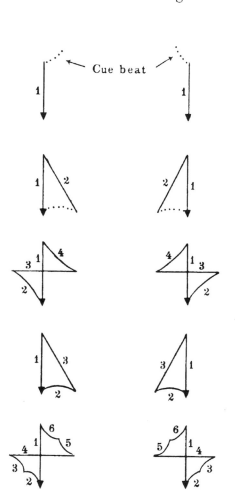

The left hand is used to indicate expression when a section, or soloist is to play, and other similar motions to convey interpretations. In playing softly small motions of the baton are used and the left palm is downward. In playing loud, vigorous strokes of the baton are used and the left palm is brought upward.

Those who are interested in conducting should obtain a good book on the subject. Take instruction from a good conductor, as written words alone can not teach conducting. And, in addition to the two mentioned, get as much actual experience in conducting as possible.

Part XVIII.

MAJOR, MINOR, AUGMENTED, AND DIMINISHED INTERVALS

The degrees of a scale are named as follows:

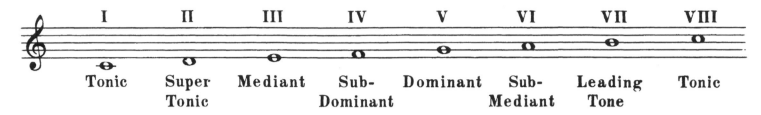

I	II	III	IV	V	VI	VII	VIII
Tonic	Super Tonic	Mediant	Sub-Dominant	Dominant	Sub-Mediant	Leading Tone	Tonic

Intervals are classified as, MAJOR, MINOR, PERFECT, DIMINISHED, or AUGMENTED.

Table of intervals—Key of C Major.

How many steps in each interval?

Prime Second Third Fourth Fifth Sixth Seventh Octave

Intervals in a major scale are further designated as major or perfect intervals.

How many steps in each interval?

| Perfect Prime | Major Second | Major Third | Perfect Fourth | Perfect Fifth | Major Sixth | Major Seventh | Perfect Octave |

Perfect and Minor intervals.

How many steps in each interval?

| Perfect Prime | Minor Second | Minor Third | Perfect Fourth | Perfect Fifth | Minor Sixth | Minor Seventh | Perfect Octave |

The word "diminished" means, made smaller.

How many steps in each interval?

"Augmented intervals" (made larger).

How many steps in each interval?

Whenever the notes forming an interval are interchanged, an **inversion** takes place. The addition of the interchanged intervals, totals nine. Major intervals become minor, and minor become major when the notes are interchanged.

A prime becomes an octave.   1 — 8

A second becomes a seventh.   2 — 7

A third becomes a sixth.   3 — 6

A fourth becomes a fifth.   4 — 5

A fifth becomes a fourth.   5 — 4

A sixth becomes a third.   6 — 3

A seventh becomes a second.   7 — 2

An octave becomes a prime.   8 — 1

What are the following intervals?

Write notes to form the following intervals.

Major third	Minor third	Perfect octave	Major sixth	Perfect fifth	Major second	Minor seventh

Minor second	Perfect fourth	Diminished third	Augmented fifth	Diminished fifth	Minor sixth

Aug. second	Dim. seventh	Dim. second	Aug. third	Major seventh	Major third

Part XIX.
CHORDS

A chord is the sounding of two or more tones, simultaneously.

A triad is a chord made up of a tone as the root or fundamental, a third, and a fifth above.

A major triad consists of a root, major third, and perfect fifth.   (A major third plus a minor third.)

A minor triad consists of a root, minor third, and perfect fifth.   (A minor third plus a major third.)

A diminished triad consists of a root, minor third and diminished fifth.   (Two minor thirds.)

An augmented triad consists of a root, major third and augmented fifth.   (Two major thirds.)

What kind of triads are the following:

Build triads on the following notes.

48

The notes of a triad may be rearranged, making it possible to write the triad in three positions.

When the root (fundamental tone) is on the bottom, the triad is in root position. When the third is the lowest note, this is called the first inversion. When the fifth is the lowest tone, the chord is in the second inversion.

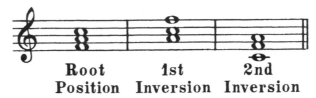

Build triads using the following notes as the lowest tone.

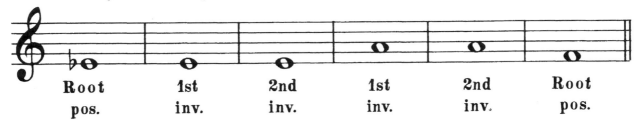

Any note of a triad may be doubled.

The chord of the seventh.

A seventh chord is formed by adding to a triad, a note a seventh above the root.

Seventh chords may be built on any degree of a scale. The most important seventh chord is built on the dominant (fifth tone) of a scale. This is called a dominant seventh.

Seventh chords may be written in the following positions.

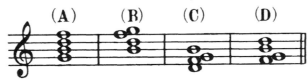

When the third is the lowest tone, the 7th chord is in the 1st inversion. When the fifth is the lowest tone, the 7th chord is in the 2nd inversion. When the seventh is the lowest tone, the 7th chord is in the 3rd inversion.

Music is played or sung in unison when all members of a group sing or play the same melody on exactly the same notes or in octaves. When a group sings or plays various pitches of various chords which blend together, the music is in harmony.

Combinations of tones in chords, inversions and progressions from one chord to another come under the study of HARMONY.